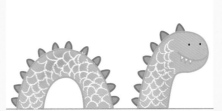

The wax crayon will resist the paint.

use two shades of tissue paper, if you have them.

4. Using bright runny paints, fill in the head and scales, but don't fill in the spikes. Leave the paint to dry, then fill in the spikes.

5. When the paint is dry, outline the spikes, body and mouth with green and orange felt-tip pens. Add black eyes, too.

6. Rip lots of pieces of blue tissue paper for the sea. Then, glue them below the pencil line, overlapping them a little, like this.

# Pop-up monster card

Make the cut about two thirds of the way down the fold.

1. Cut two rectangles of paper the same size, one white and one yellow. Fold them both in half, with the short ends together.

2. Make a cut into the fold in the white rectangle, for the monster's mouth. Fold back the paper on each side of the cut, like this.

3. Turn the card over and fold the flaps back on themselves. Then, unfold the flaps, so that the card lies flat again.

If you make the cut a third of the way down the fold in step 2, you can draw a whole monster.

Write a message around your monster or on the back of the card.

Glue the teeth to the back of the flaps.

Line up the folds.

4. Open the card a little, then push the flaps down through the fold, like this. Close the card and press the folds to flatten them.

5. Open the card. Draw a monster around the mouth and fill it in with felt-tip pens. Then, cut teeth from paper and glue them on.

6. Cut around the monster. Then, spread glue all over the back of it, except for the mouth. Press it onto the yellow rectangle.

You could make a monster with lots of teeth.

# Stand-up monsters

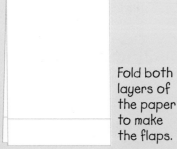

Fold both layers of the paper to make the flaps.

Don't draw on the flap.

1. Fold a long rectangle of thick white paper in half, like this. Fold the bottom up to make flaps for the base, then unfold it again.

2. Draw the head at the top of the paper. Add the body, stopping a little way above the flap. Then, draw lots of lines for bandages.

3. Draw over all the lines with a black felt-tip pen. Add paler shadows next to the outlines and bandages. Then, fill in the teeth, too.

You can make your stand-up monster any shape you like, as long as you don't cut along the fold at the top.

To make a monster with separate legs, make four cuts into the flap in step 4.

Don't cut along this part of the fold.

4. Make two cuts up into the flap, one below each leg. Then, cut out the monster, leaving a thin white border around it.

5. Fold the flaps inside the monster to make the base. Then, stand the monster on a piece of black paper and draw around the base.

6. Lift off the monster and cut out the shape you have drawn. Glue the shape on top of the flaps inside the monster, like this.

Try making a monster that looks like a kind of animal, such as an octopus or a wolf.

# Monster finger puppet

## Step 1

Use a pencil.

1. Draw the monster's head on a piece of white paper. Add horns and a face, then draw a rounded shape for the body.

Push your fingers through the holes in the monster's body, then push on the monster's feet.

Try making a monster with a long tail.

## Step 2

Leave white spots.

2. Add arms at the sides of the body. Draw a shape for the tummy, too. Then, fill in the monster using felt-tip pens.

## Step 3

3. Using a thin black pen, draw lots of short lines on all the outlines, to make thick scratchy lines. Then, cut out the monster.

## Step 4

4. Lay the monster on a piece of thin cardboard. Draw around it with a pencil, then cut out the shape you have drawn.

## Step 5

5. Draw two circles near the bottom of the shape, for your fingers. Cut up into the circles, then carefully cut around them.

## Step 6

6. Spread glue on the shape, stopping just above the holes. Then, press the monster on top, lining up the edges of both shapes.

## Step 7

7. For the monster's feet, draw a foot on thick paper, making the leg part as wide as two fingers, like this. Cut out the shape.

You could make a monster with more than two legs.

Use white paper.

Tab

8. Fold a piece of paper in half. Lay the foot on it and draw around it. Then, turn the foot over and draw around it again, like this.

9. Draw a tab on the side of one of the legs. Hold the layers together and cut around the shape, including the tab.

10. Fold the feet in half, then fold and glue the tabs inside them. Then, fill in the feet with felt-tip pens and add black outlines.

9

# Monster plants

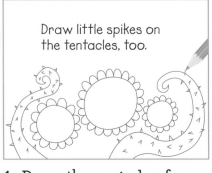

Draw little spikes on the tentacles, too.

1. Draw three circles for the monsters' heads on a piece of thick white paper. Add petals around them, then draw some tentacles.

2. Add grass at the bottom of the drawing. Then, use a clean paintbrush to brush water over the monsters, tentacles and grass.

3. Blob watery green and yellow paints onto the wet paper, so that they bleed into each other. Leave the paint to dry completely.

You could add
flies between the
monster plants.

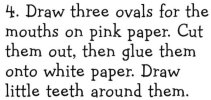 

4. Draw three ovals for the mouths on pink paper. Cut them out, then glue them onto white paper. Draw little teeth around them.

5. Cut around the teeth and mouths, then fold the teeth in, onto the mouths. Turn the mouths over and spread glue on the back.

6. Press the mouths onto the monsters and bend up the teeth. Then, draw over all the outlines with a black pen and add eyes.

To make a snapping monster, draw an open mouth shape in step 4.

To make a monster with more feet, tape on extra pieces of drinking straw in step 4.

You could make a monster with pointed shoes or boots.

# Dangly monster

Use a pencil.

1. Draw a circle for the monster's head on a piece of thick paper. Add eyes, a mouth and horns, then draw a simple body.

2. Draw two hands and two feet on the paper. Then, draw thick lines over all the pencil lines with a black pencil.

3. Using yellow and green pencils, fill in the monster's head and body. Fill in the hands and feet, too. Then, cut out all the shapes.

Try drawing a monster that looks like a skeleton.

Pull one of the monster's feet to make its legs different lengths.

Hang the monster up, using the loop.

4. Turn the monster over, then cut two short pieces from a drinking straw. Tape one at the top of the body and one at the bottom.

5. Cut two pieces of string or thread for the monster's arms and legs. Thread them through the pieces of drinking straw, like this.

6. Lay the hands and feet face down, then tape them onto the ends of the pieces of thread. Tape a loop of thread onto the head, too.

13

# Undersea monsters

Really fine glitter
works best.

1. Lay a piece of thick
black paper on a piece of
thick cardboard. Tape down
all the edges, like this, to
keep it flat.

2. Brush thick white glue
all over the black paper.
Gently sprinkle glitter all
over the wet glue, then
leave it to dry.

3. Mix a little white paint into thick purple and pink paints. Paint a big purple 'C' shape for a monster's body on the black paper.

4. Add circles above the body for eyes. Join them onto the body with curved lines, then add tentacles at the end of the body.

5. Paint a pink teardrop shape for a little monster. Add a round eye on each side, then paint fins and a tail. Leave the paint to dry.

An undersea monster can be any shape you like – look at this picture for ideas.

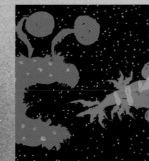

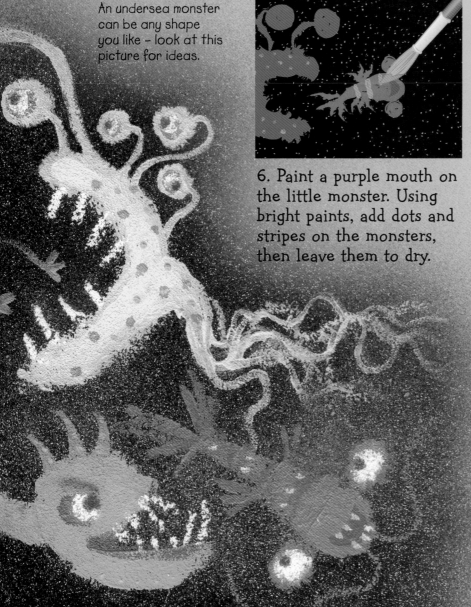

6. Paint a purple mouth on the little monster. Using bright paints, add dots and stripes on the monsters, then leave them to dry.

7. Use a white chalk pastel or chalk to add eyes and teeth. Then, add more tentacles and feelers with bright pastels, like this.

8. Draw dark dots on the eyes for pupils. Add more dots and stripes on the monsters. Then, peel the paper off the cardboard.

# Swarming flying monsters

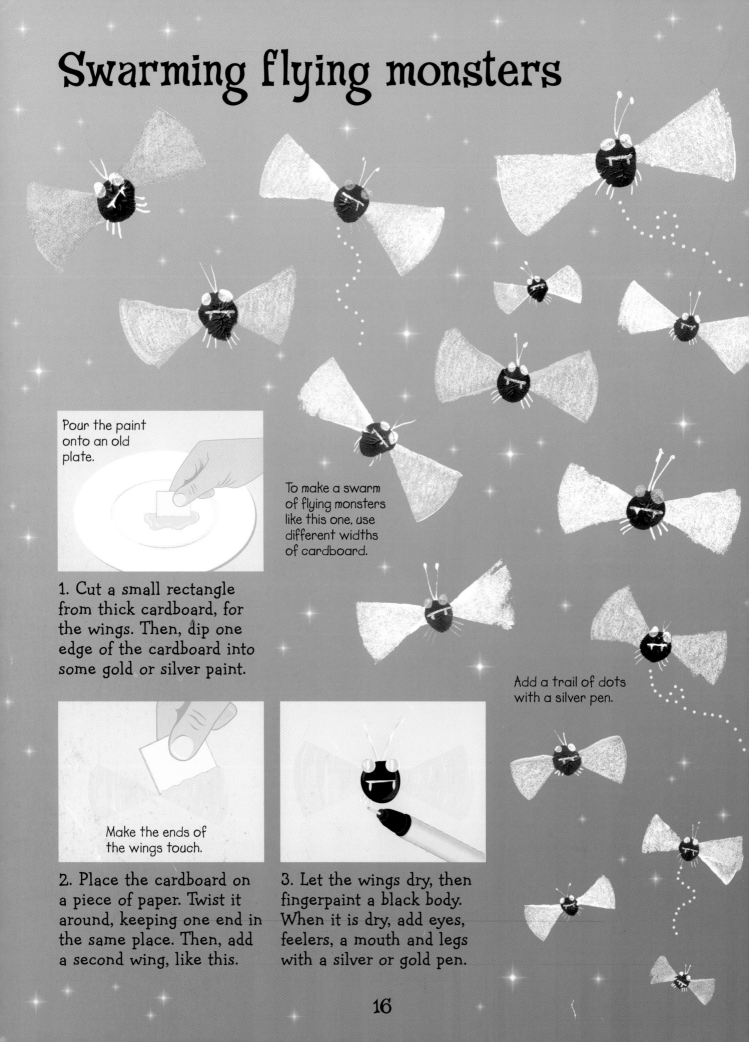

Pour the paint onto an old plate.

To make a swarm of flying monsters like this one, use different widths of cardboard.

1. Cut a small rectangle from thick cardboard, for the wings. Then, dip one edge of the cardboard into some gold or silver paint.

Make the ends of the wings touch.

2. Place the cardboard on a piece of paper. Twist it around, keeping one end in the same place. Then, add a second wing, like this.

3. Let the wings dry, then fingerpaint a black body. When it is dry, add eyes, feelers, a mouth and legs with a silver or gold pen.

Add a trail of dots with a silver pen.

# Jellybean monsters

1. Using a pencil, draw a curved bean shape for the monster's body on a piece of white paper. Then, add long arms and short legs.

2. Draw two round eyes, a blob for a nose and a toothy grin near the top of the body. Then, add two little horns.

3. Fill in the monster with felt-tip pens, leaving his eyes and teeth white. Then, draw over all the lines with a thin black pen.

You could draw lots of monsters in different positions.

For a laughing monster, draw 'V' shapes for eyes and a big open mouth.

# Sparkly monster

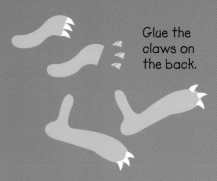

Glue the claws on the back.

1. Draw a shape for the monster's body on green paper and add a mouth. Cut out the body, then lay it on a piece of pink paper.

2. Draw around the body, then lift it off. Draw a tummy on the pink shape and cut it out. Then, glue the tummy onto the body.

3. Draw arms and legs on green paper, then cut them out. Cut claws from shiny paper, then glue them onto the arms and legs.

Glue the triangles shiny-side down.

4. Glue an arm and a leg onto the back of the body. Glue the others onto the front. Draw eyes, then cut them out and glue them on.

5. Cut triangles for spikes from shiny paper, then cut smaller ones for teeth. Turn the monster over and glue on all the triangles.

6. Cut lots of different-sized circles from bright and shiny papers. Don't worry if the circles aren't completely round.

You could glue tiny beads onto the circles, too.

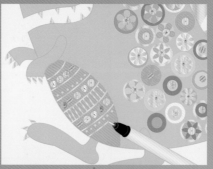

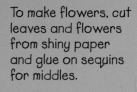

To make flowers, cut leaves and flowers from shiny paper and glue on sequins for middles.

7. Glue the circles onto the monster, layering smaller ones on top of larger ones. Then, glue sequins on top of some of the circles.

8. Glue lines of sequins on the tummy, then draw patterns on it with a gold pen. Draw lines and spots on some of the circles, too.

You could use stickers from the sticker pages to decorate your monster.

To make a hill, glue on a curved paper shape in step 6 and glue your monster on top.

# Monster bookmark

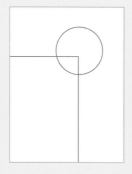

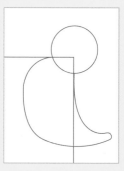

1. Lay a book on the bottom left-hand corner of a piece of thick white paper. Draw around it with a pencil, pressing lightly.

2. Lift off the book. Then, draw a circle for the monster's head over the top right-hand corner of the rectangle, like this.

3. Draw a shape for the body, following the top and right-hand side of the rectangle. Then, add a pointed tail at the bottom.

To make your monster grip onto a book, slide him between the pages, leaving his hands outside.

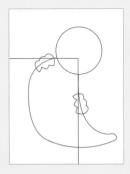

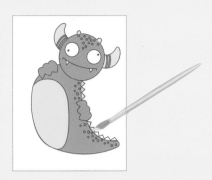

4. Draw a hand at the top of the body, near the head. Make it overlap the body. Then, add another hand just above the tail, like this.

5. Erase the rectangle and any lines inside the hands. Then, draw the monster's face and horns, and add a big oval tummy.

6. Draw spots on the body and head. Add stripes on the horns, and fins on his back, too. Then, fill in the monster with paints.

To make a bookmark like this one, just cut around one hand.

7. When the paint is dry, draw over all the lines and around the spots with a black felt-tip pen. Then, cut out the monster.

Make sure you don't cut off his hands completely.

8. To make your monster into a bookmark, cut part of the way around each of his hands, along the red lines shown here.

# Monster mask

1. Draw a large egg shape for the monster's head on a piece of thick paper. Make the shape wider and taller than your head.

2. Draw a wide curving mouth halfway down the head. Add two pointed ears and two little bumps near the top, like this.

3. Cut out the monster's head. Then, carefully push the point of a ballpoint pen through the middle of the mouth, to make a hole.

 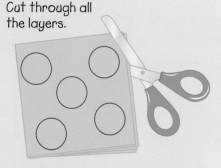 

Cut through all the layers.

This is the back of the mask.

4. Push one blade of a pair of scissors through the hole. Cut to the edge of the mouth, then cut all the way around it.

5. Fold a piece of paper in half. Fold it in half again, then draw five spots on it. Cut out the spots and glue them all over the mask.

6. Draw rounded teeth on white paper and cut them out. Turn the mask over, then glue the teeth around the mouth, like this.

  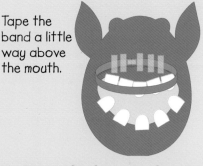

Tape the band a little way above the mouth.

7. Draw two big eyes on paper and cut them out. Then, cut two long strips of thick paper and fold over one end of each one.

8. Fold the strips one way and then the other to make zigzags. Glue an eye onto each one, then glue the other ends onto the mask.

9. Cut a thick paper band that fits around your head, with a little overlap. Tape the ends, then tape it onto the back of the mask.

You can't see the zigzag springs in this photograph, but they will make the eyes bounce around when you wear your mask.

To wear your mask, slide the band onto your head and look out through the mouth.

You could make monster hands to wear with your mask (see pages 24-25).

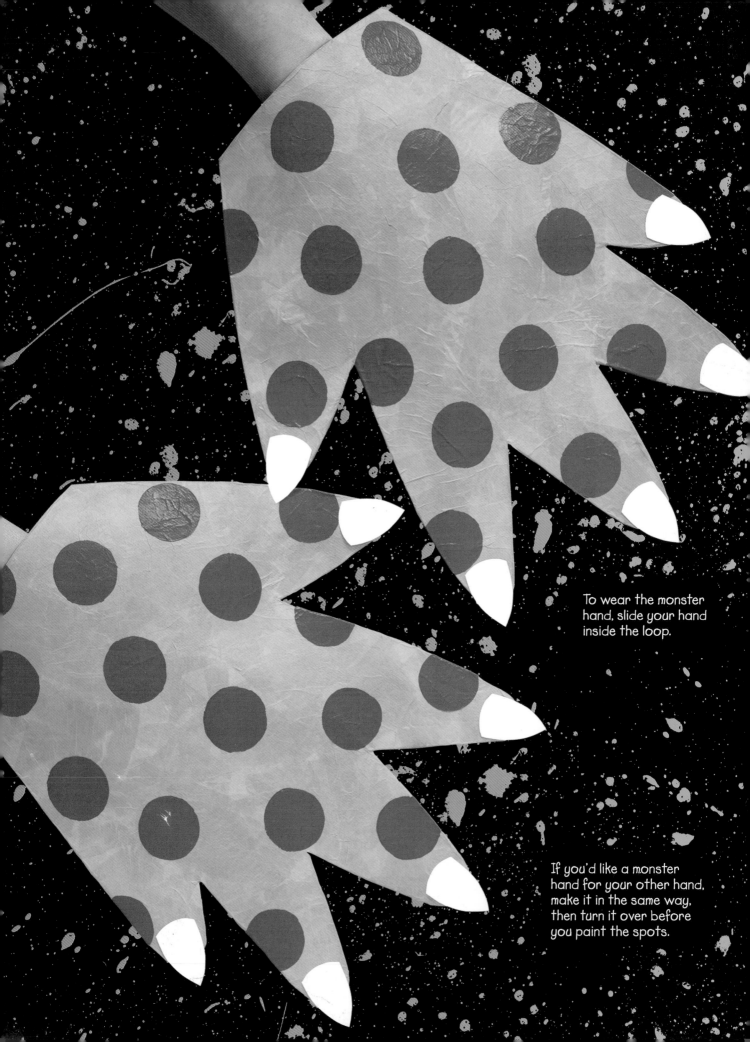

To wear the monster hand, slide your hand inside the loop.

If you'd like a monster hand for your other hand, make it in the same way, then turn it over before you paint the spots.

# Monster hand

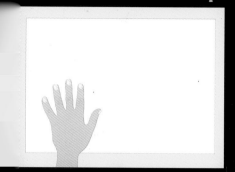

1. Lay your hand over the edge of a large piece of thin cardboard. The edge of the cardboard needs to be level with your wrist.

Make the big hand wide at the bottom.

2. Carefully draw around your hand with a pencil. Then, draw a much bigger hand around the outline you have just drawn.

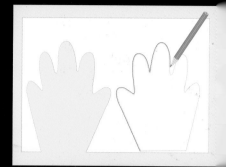

3. Cut out the big hand, then turn it over and lay it back on the cardboard, like this. Draw around it, then cut out the second shape.

Don't wrap it around too tightly.

4. Cut a strip of cardboard that will wrap once around your hand, with a small overlap. Then, tape the end down to make a loop.

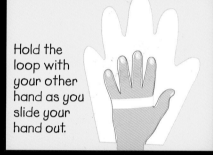

Hold the loop with your other hand as you slide your hand out.

5. Lay your hand inside the outline on the first big hand, then slide it out of the loop. Tape the loop onto the cardboard hand.

Try not to squash the loop inside.

6. Lay the other cardboard hand on top. Lining up the edges as well as you can, tape them together, but leave the bottom open.

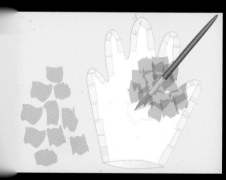

7. Rip lots of pieces of green tissue paper. Then, brush white glue on part of the hand and press on pieces of tissue paper.

8. Brush on more glue and press on more tissue paper until the hand is covered. When the glue is dry, paint pink spots on the hand.

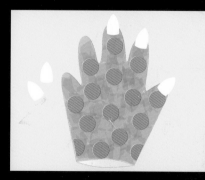

9. Leave the paint to dry. Then, cut five fingernails from white cardboard. Glue one nail onto the end of each finger, like this.

# Swamp monster

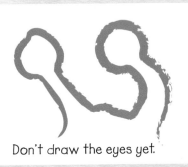

Don't draw the eyes yet.

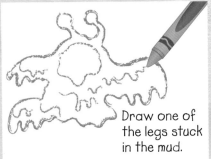

Draw one of the legs stuck in the mud.

1. Using a brown wax crayon, draw two stalks for the monster's eyes. Join the stalks at the bottom with a curved line.

2. Draw wobbly arms, the sides of the body, and legs. Draw a mouth, then add wobbly lines for mud on the monster's body.

3. Use a green wax crayon to draw a line for the edge of the swamp. Draw green grass above the line, and brown grass below it.

The wax resists the paint.

4. Brush watery brown paint all over the monster and above the line of the swamp. Brush watery green paint below the line.

5. Dab green and brown paint on the patches of grass. Let the paint dry, then fill in the monster with darker brown paint.

26

You could draw a big swamp with lots of monsters in it.

6. When the paint is dry, use thick yellow paint to add pointed teeth and circles for the eyes. Then, leave the paint to dry.

7. Fill in the mouth with pencils. Use a brown pencil to outline the teeth and eyes, then add eyebrows and pupils.

8. Draw lines for mud in the swamp with the brown wax crayon. Then, add cans or bottles above the lines with pencils.

# Wobbling monster

You don't need the egg white or yolk.

1. Tap the middle of an egg sharply on the rim of a mug to crack it. Use your fingers to carefully break the egg in half over the mug.

The weight of the poster tack will make the monster stand up.

2. Wash the eggshell, then let it dry. Using white glue, glue a ball of poster tack into the middle of the bottom half of the shell.

3. Leave the glue to dry completely. Then, cut several small, thin pieces of bright tissue paper and brush glue all over them.

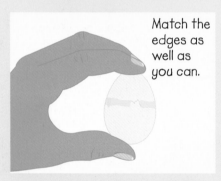

Match the edges as well as you can.

4. Hold the bottom of the eggshell and gently lay the other half on top. Then, press the pieces of tissue paper over the join.

5. Rip more tissue paper into lots of pieces. Brush part of the egg with glue, then press pieces of tissue paper onto the glue.

Lay the egg on a piece of plastic foodwrap.

6. Brush on more glue and press on more pieces of tissue paper, until the egg is covered. Then, leave the glue to dry completely.

Push your monster over, then watch him wobble until he stands up again.

Use a thin paintbrush.

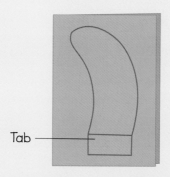

Tab

The tabs need to be at the back.

7. Draw eyes and a mouth on the egg with a pencil. Paint them with white and black paints. Let them dry, then add pupils and teeth.

8. For the horns, fold a small piece of thick paper in half. Draw a curved shape, then add a tab at the bottom, like this.

9. Holding the layers of paper together, cut out the horns, including the tab. Fold over the tabs and glue them onto the monster.

You could paint spots on your monster.

To make an angry monster like the one below, paint a down-turned mouth with pointed teeth.

These different-sized monsters were made with a mixture of hens', quails' and ducks' eggs.

# Hide-and-seek monsters

1. Draw a square on a piece of paper, for the doors of the wardrobe that the monster will hide inside. Then, cut out the square.

2. Fold the left edge in to the middle of the square and crease the fold well. Then, fold the right edge over to meet the left edge.

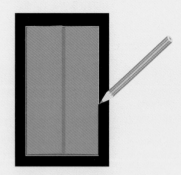

3. Lay the folded doors on a piece of black paper. Then, draw around them with a pencil, as close to the edges as you can.

Line up the edges and the folds.

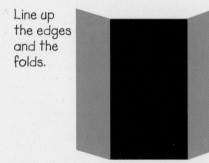

4. Lift off the folded square and open the doors. Then, cut out the black rectangle. Glue it inside the open doors, like this.

5. Shut the doors again and turn the paper over. Spread glue on the back, then press it onto another piece of paper.

6. Draw a shape for a wardrobe around the doors and cut it out. Then, cut little circles for door handles and glue them on.

Make the monster small enough to hide in the wardrobe.

7. For the monster, draw an oval body and an arm on bright paper. Cut out the shapes, then glue the arm onto the back of the body.

8. Cut two circles from white paper for the eyes. Add spots for pupils with a black pen. Then, glue the eyes onto the monster.

9. Cut a mouth and fangs from paper and glue them onto the monster. Then, glue the monster inside the wardrobe, like this.

You could hide a monster in any piece of furniture, behind curtains or even under a rug.

Toys

# Little round monsters

You could draw a monster with tentacles instead of legs.

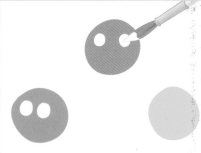

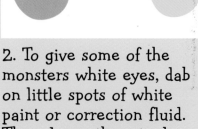

**1.** For the monsters' bodies, draw lots of circles with different bright felt-tip pens. Leave spaces between the circles.

**2.** To give some of the monsters white eyes, dab on little spots of white paint or correction fluid. Then, leave them to dry.

**3.** Draw arms and legs on the monsters with a black felt-tip pen. Make the arms and legs lots of different shapes.

**4.** Draw eyes and mouths on the monsters. Add lots of little teeth. Then, draw pointed horns, tails, wings and spikes, too.

You can draw any number of arms, legs or eyes on your monster.

Try drawing some eyes on stalks.

Photographic manipulation: John Russell